Mana

Making Time

Kate Keenan

RAVETTE BOOKS

Published by Ravette Books Limited
P.O. Box 296
Horsham
West Sussex RH13 8FH
Tel & Fax: (01 403) 711443

Series Editor – Anne Tauté
Editor – Catriona Scott

Cover design – Jim Wire
Printing & Binding – Cox & Wyman Ltd.
Production – Oval Projects Ltd.

An Oval Project
produced for Ravette Books.

Cover – Imprecise time is the resort of those
who could do better at managing it.

Acknowledgments and thanks to:
Barry Tuckwood
Jeremy Bethell

Contents

Making Time   5

1. Wasting Time   6

2. Planning Your Tasks   15

3. Scheduling Your Time   24

4. Ways of Saving Time   32

5. Working With Others   41

6. Making Time for Yourself   51

Check List for Making Time   56

The Benefits of Making Time   58

Glossary   60

This book is dedicated to
those who would like to manage better
but are too busy to begin.

Making Time

Time is a finite commodity. To literally 'make time' is not possible; however, you can certainly get more done in the time available. Once time has been spent, it can never be recovered. Once it has gone, you have even less time to do what you want to do.

Each of us has the same amount of time available. Most of us admit that we do not have enough time, yet some people seem to manage to get more done than others. It is vital to understand why this is the case.

To save time, you have to spend a little time. If you do not take time to work out what you are trying to achieve on a daily basis, you will only waste more time.

This book looks at how time can be wasted and what you can do, if not to make more of it then, at least, to make the most of it.

1. Wasting Time

Nobody likes to think that they waste time, but not only is it easy to do so, half the time you may not even realize you are doing it. Here are some examples:

- Going over the same ground twice because you have forgotten something the first time round.

- Only achieving half of what you had planned for the day and not knowing why.

- Wondering whatever happened to the best part of the day.

- Seeing your list of things 'to do' getting longer and longer.

- Seeing your 'pending' tray get larger.

- Not being able to find an important piece of paper when you need it.

- Spending time looking for something in the wrong place because you have forgotten you put it somewhere else.

Many of these symptoms relate to self-organization. In the short-term, most of us can get away with not being too well organized. In the longer-term, it will end up as a serious problem.

What is Getting in the Way

Working out how to make effective use of your time requires you to examine some of the things which are getting in the way.

Much of the secret of managing time has to do with how well organized you are. If you have a low regard for administrative procedures, you will probably find the idea of being organized rather a nuisance. In fact, being well organized will help you save large amounts of time – always provided you do not become so obsessed with the systems to save time, that once again, you waste it.

Finding the Cause

To manage time well, you need to be honest with yourself. Ask yourself these questions and answer them as truthfully as you can.

1. What do I do that need not be done at all?

2. What do I do that could and should be done by someone else?

3. What do I do that is taking longer than it should?

4. What do I do that wastes other people's time?

1. Doing things that need not be done at all is a very common way of wasting time. You are not only producing things which you do not need, you could also be producing things which no-one else needs. For example:

- You (or others) are still doing something unnecessary because it has always been done that way since anyone can remember. Do you know what happens to this work? Is the output genuinely useful to yourself, or others, or does it simply get filed or stored and never looked at again?

- You have several sets of books into which transactions are laboriously entered.

- You are still running a manual system after it has been computerized simply because you do not trust the new system.

All these activities are wasting time.

2. Doing something that could and should be done by someone else is tempting, especially when it is work which you are, or have been, good at. But if you do not delegate certain tasks you will have less time to devote to managing. It often seems quicker to do something yourself than to spend time delegating it, and even when you have delegated a task you may find it difficult to resist the temptation to keep stepping in at the slightest hint of a difficulty. But if you do, you face further time-wasting situations because:

- You will be spending your time doing something which someone else is meant to do.

- People will learn very quickly that if they have a problem you will sort it for them.

- You cannot do the tasks you should be doing.

What is more, many will resent your help, while others will cease to bother trying in the first place.

In the meantime, your own efficiency is at risk and you may end up having to delegate tasks you are responsible for to those who cannot do them well enough – and who then need you to help them once more.

3. Things may be taking longer because:

- You are not personally organized and cannot find all the relevant things you require to complete the job.

- You find the task demanding because you have not taken the time to inform yourself properly.

- You rush into action before you have worked out exactly what it is you need to do.

- You are doing it all yourself.

4. Nobody likes to admit that they **waste other people's time**. Most people will say they never have enough time of their own, so how can they possibly waste other people's? But think about:

- Having second thoughts after people have already done a great deal of work.

- Forgetting to pass on new information so people are still working on old, out-of-date information.

- Asking people to see you about something and then neglecting to have the relevant papers or material to hand, so you waste time looking for them.

- Holding impromptu meetings that have no agenda, so people do not know what the meeting is about and cannot prepare themselves.

- Allowing interruptions so that discussion lasts much longer than it should and is less effective.

- Keeping punctual people waiting (with or without an explanation) because you are running late.

If you plead guilty to any of these, think how much time in total is being lost through your actions. For example: if your lack of preparation for a meeting of 10 people means that it lasts 25 minutes longer than necessary, you have wasted a total of 250 minutes which is more than half a working day.

Excuses

If a task is taking a long time because you find it difficult, you will not be able to do all that is required of you, so you will end up falling behind. If you are avoiding that task, it will not go away and will ultimately end up as a self-imposed crisis – and crises are prize methods of wasting time.

There are plenty of plausible reasons for not being able to get things done on time. But as everyone has the same amount of time at their disposal, it must be the way individuals manage time which makes the difference. In fact, there is no such thing as not having enough time to do something. One can always make time. What is missing is the inclination.

The next time you find yourself or others saying "I haven't got time..." think about why you or they don't want to do it. Who wouldn't find the time to attend a champagne reception in Paris?

People fail to get things done on time because:

- The task does not appear to be worth making much of an effort for.

- Inactivity does not seem to have any serious immediate penalties.

- There are more interesting things to do than the task in hand.

● It is easy to forget how to get things done on time.

If you fool yourself into believing your own excuses for not doing things, you will never get down to doing something about it. Be honest with yourself and identify the real reasons why things either do not get done at all or do not get finished on time.

Ask yourself how satisfied you are with the way you use the time you have available. It may be that you are reasonably effective but feel you could do more. Very probably the things you are not getting done on time are those you may not want to do or find more difficult to tackle. A useful strategy here is to make a record of how you are currently spending your time. This gives you an objective bench mark against which to measure your progress in managing time.

Summary: Your Attitude

Your attitude will reflect whether you want to be positive in managing time or whether you want to use time as an excuse for being ineffective.

It requires the will on your part to put things right. Once you have made the decision to do better, the rest is comparatively easy.

Questions to Ask Yourself

To assess whether you are managing your time effectively, think about your answers to the following questions:

➤ Do I find it difficult to say what I have done during a day?

➤ Do I find meeting deadlines a problem?

➤ Do I do things which really do not need to be done?

➤ Do I tend to take over other people's work for them?

➤ Do I tend to take longer than I should on certain tasks?

➤ Do I find it difficult to be on time for appointments?

➤ Do I often forget what I was going to do?

If you have answered 'Yes' to most of these questions, your ability to manage time probably requires some attention.

You Will Be Doing Better If...

★ You spend a little time to think about how you use your time.

★ You can identify some of the things you are doing that waste your time.

★ You can identify some of the things you may be doing which wastes other people's time.

★ You can recognize which reasons are really excuses for not completing something, or for not doing something at all.

★ You can clearly indicate your main achievements at the end of each day.

★ You have a positive attitude towards wanting to manage your time.

2.   Planning Your Tasks

Churchill once said that if you want a thing done, you should give it to a busy person. Busy people seem better at controlling time than others. They seem to be able to cram more things into their day than anyone else. Because these people are busy, they will always find a way to fit what is required into their schedule. The reasons for this may be because:

- They have a sense of urgency about getting things done.

- They take deadlines seriously and do not like missing them.

- They have developed the skills required to achieve things on time.

- They are fully aware of what they are responsible for producing.

Knowing Your Responsibilities

In business, every job has a job title and, by implication, a job description that outlines those areas for which you are personally responsible.

It is by being fully aware of what you are there to do that you can identify what you should be doing and compare this with what you are actually doing.

If you do not have a job description, it is a good idea to construct one for yourself. Identify the main responsibilities of your job. Make a list of the tasks you need to accomplish to do the work effectively. Think carefully about what the real scope of your job is, and how it contributes to the overall effectiveness of your business or profession.

You may find you do certain things which are not central to ensuring effective performance in your work. They may be fun and enjoyable, but you need to recognize they are not the core tasks for which you are being paid.

The first step in making more time is to clearly understand what your responsibilities are; what it is that you are there for. Once you have understood this, it is far easier to establish your goals and identify where your priorities lie.

Setting Goals

Setting and achieving goals plays a major part in managing time. If you do not know what you have to do, you will not know where to start.

Knowing what is important and needs to be done puts you in control of events rather than events being in control of you. This way you stand a chance of achieving what is required of you in the time you have available. Goals are useful. They help you to:

- Focus your attention on where you are going.

- Plan what to do within a given time-frame.

- Help others understand what is happening and how they fit into the scheme.

Knowing your goals prevents you from wasting time. To set goals effectively you need to:

- Work out what you want to achieve.

- Discuss your thoughts with someone else.

- Write down what you resolve to do.

Identifying Priorities

It will help you achieve your goals if you identify your priorities. To do this, look at your workload as a whole and decide which activities are top priority. These can be categorized under four headings:

- **Essential tasks** – ones which if you did not perform, you would not fulfil your role effectively.

- **Tasks which you should perform** provided the top priority tasks are being carried out.

- **Tasks you would like to do** in the fullness of time. These are usually the things that never get done.

- **Tasks that have a low priority** but which are easy and fun. These usually get done first.

List the tasks facing you under these four headings. Look at your list and assign time to what you need to do, what you should do, and what you would like to do. This helps you to eliminate activities which you like doing, but which are not essential. It also allows you to decide to do a non-essential, but enjoyable, task from time to time in the full knowledge that it is not high priority, but that you are doing it as a reward for doing longer, more complex tasks.

Once you have identified where your priorities lie, try not to stick so rigidly to them that you cannot change course if circumstances should dictate. Be flexible: situations can change dramatically and cause your current priorities to become irrelevant. Sticking to them in these circumstances can only waste time.

However, should a priority activity disappear (for instance, a meeting is cancelled) watch out that you do not simply fritter the time away. Use the energy you had activated for that task to tackle another of the tasks on your list.

Urgent and Important

Understanding the difference between what is urgent and what is important plays a significant part in making time.

Things which are **urgent** are pressing in their need for attention, but they may be trivial; for example, sorting out the car parking arrangements. Things that are **important** require careful consideration and usually take extra time to think about; for example, your business plan for the next quarter.

Urgent things have a habit of looking important because of their time constraints. They require quick reactions, but they should not take up much time. You may have to put off something which is urgent to attend to something which is important.

There may also be occasions when putting off important things in order to do something more immediately interesting is fine, provided you do it on purpose. If you want to take time to do something of this sort, work out how to recoup the time, then you can enjoy doing it without guilt or remorse.

There are, of course, some things that are both urgent and important. When both apply, the matter requires your fullest attention. There is no question of doing something more appealing first. The penalty will be that you run out of time.

Types of Task

Think about the nature of the things you do. Consider how much of your time is taken up with executive activities and how much time is spent performing day-to-day tasks specific to your business or profession.

Managing tasks will involve you in the following:

- Thinking ahead to ensure you have all you need to run things efficiently and effectively.

- Having the right people and the right materials in the right place at the right time.

- Telling people what to do and the standard they should be achieving, and if necessary, advising them how to do it.

- Making sure that relevant people know what is going on and what they have to do to ensure that things go well.

– i.e. planning, organizing, directing and controlling.

Look at your list of priorities. If you are not performing any of the above key functions to any great degree, analyse what it is that you are in fact doing and how it fits in with your key responsibilities.

You may find that you are letting others off-load tasks which they find difficult on to you because you are better at them than they are. Or it could be that you are held up at work because of a lack of the right systems or equipment. Most of all, you may not have realized that it is your competence in executive tasks which makes a real contribution to saving time.

Summary: No Time to Lose

By identifying your responsibilities, knowing what your goals are, putting your tasks in order of priority, and being able to distinguish between those tasks that are urgent and those that are important, you will find it easier to plan how to use your time more effectively.

If this all sounds a bit exacting and time-consuming, it is worth considering the story of the Chinese Emperor. He indicated to his estate manager that he would like an avenue of cedar trees to lead up to his palace. The manager objected. "It will take 300 years for this project to come to fruition", he pointed out. "Well," said the Emperor, "you haven't got a minute to lose."

Questions to Ask Yourself

Think about how you go about planning your time and answer the following questions:

➤ Do I fully understand what are my responsibilities and what are not my responsibilities?

➤ Am I clear about my goals?

➤ Have I identified where my priorities lie?

➤ Do I know what I should achieve today, if I do nothing else?

➤ Can I distinguish between what is important and what is urgent?

➤ Am I working on the right type of tasks to make more effective use of my time?

You Will Be Doing Better If...

★ You identify your essential tasks.

★ You identify your goals.

★ You get your important work done within a pre-determined time-scale.

★ You understand the need to be flexible when priorities change unexpectedly.

★ You distinguish between urgent and important work.

★ You carry out the right sort of executive tasks which assist you to manage your time better.

★ You resolve to start planning your time right away.

3.   Scheduling Your Time

Organizing your time would be easier if other people did not always want things from you so that you never seem to get your own work finished. Whatever the day brings or the world outside demands, you need to develop a range of strategies to help you make the best use of your time.

Dealing with Deadlines

Parkinson's Law states that work expands to fill the time available for its completion. This is why having deadlines is important. Without them, very little tends to happen within a sensible time-frame.

External deadlines are there to ensure the success of a project. By working back from the deadline you can determine when you have to start – usually yesterday. If the deadlines imposed upon you are very tight, set your own deadlines within them – like a box within a box. This prevents you from allowing a task to fill all the time you have available.

Put a time limit on various activities by setting your watch, travel alarm or computer clock, to indicate when your time is up. You will be surprised how this concentrates the mind and how much you get done in the time you have allocated. What is more, as you get used to working within set time limits, you will find yourself completing work in less and less time.

Tackling Large Tasks

Large tasks appear daunting and can lead to inactivity simply because you do not know where to start. For example, if it fell to you to arrange the relocation of the office, it is important you are not intimidated by the complexity of the task.

The trick is to confront all large jobs by treating them as you would treat watermelons: cut them into manageable chunks. Having done so, work out a schedule for these chunks and tackle one bit at a time. By doing this, the large task appears to be perfectly possible and you can plot your progress against your schedule.

Setting Undisturbed Time

Certain things need your undivided attention and you should set aside uninterrupted time to do these things. Many people achieve this by finding another, quieter place to work, but there are several other ways to prevent interruptions by organizing 'exclusive' time:

- Have times when you are available and times when you are not to be disturbed – and tell people which are which.

- Set your answering machine to take messages for an hour or two when you are in fact there. This gives you space to get essential work done. You can deal with the messages one after the other at a chosen time.

- Install a 'white board' with waterproof pens in your bathroom, so that you can write and plan in peace.

- Keep a notebook bedside your bed. It is extraordinary how many times an important thought occurs when you are at your most relaxed.

Making the Most of Meetings

How often have you said on emerging from a meeting: "That meeting was a complete waste of time"? For example, regular weekly meetings may have become a white elephant without anyone noticing. But meetings need not waste time. So if you take charge of any, make sure you know:

- Why anyone needs to be meeting, rather than sending a memo or telephoning.

- Who should attend and why.

- What precise topics you will be discussing.

- What you want to achieve from the meeting.

Every person attending should know these things in advance if the meeting is to be productive. So if a good deal of your time is taken up by attending meetings, make sure you know:
  - the purpose of the meeting;
  - your role in it;
  - what you are required to do after it.

If you do not know these three things, question why you are going to the meeting in the first place; and whether you need to be present for the whole meeting, or simply be there to make your own contribution and learn the rest from the Minutes.

There are circumstances when a face-to-face meeting is a necessary part of the business, e.g.

- When the situation is so involved that evaluating body language will be as important (if not more so) than verbal communication.

- When you have not met before.

- When you need to consult about documents, or work with certain equipment.

Otherwise, it be could more beneficial to telephone, fax, or set up teleconferencing facilities.

Using Journey Time Effectively

Making a journey is often related to attending meetings and has equal potential in the time-wasting stakes. Always question the purpose of making journeys. If you like to travel on business, or you are faced with a journey, make the most of this 'dead' time:

- Take a PC or personal organizer with you and do some work, turning off the beeps.

- Use a dictaphone, quietly and discreetly, to deal with correspondence.

- Travel with a colleague and talk shop, being careful about how much detail you reveal.

- Clear out your brief case, making sure you take your 'litter' back to the office shredder, in a plastic bag if necessary.

- Dig out receipts from your pockets, wallet and brief case and collate them for expenses claims.

- Listen to a management tape, a talking book, or a language course.

- Think about strategy, formulate plans and make notes for future reference.

- Read those things you have meant to read for ages.

Summary: Apportioning Time

If you can schedule time for your work in a way which allows you to get things done, you will be more able to meet your deadlines. You will have set aside the time to do what you need to do, and you will find that you have made time to do all sorts of things you never had time for.

By deliberately working to self-imposed time limits which prevent time for one thing over-running and leaking into the time allocated to something else, you will be making the best of the time available.

You will also feel more confident that you are better at making time work for you, rather than being over-taken by it. This gives you the assurance that you are in charge of your working life and that you can achieve the endless numbers of things required of you on time.

Questions to Ask Yourself

Think about how you schedule your time and answer these questions:

➤ Am I meeting my deadlines?

➤ Have I broken down large tasks into their component parts?

➤ Have I got a method of setting aside uninterrupted time so as to get important things completed?

➤ Am I getting the best out of the meetings I attend?

➤ Are all my journeys necessary?

➤ Do I plan how I will use the time I have available when I make long-distance journeys?

➤ Am I scheduling my activities efficiently and making best use of the time I have at my disposal?

You Will Be Doing Better If...

★ You meet deadlines by imposing your own.

★ You use a number of positive ways to have uninterrupted time.

★ You tackle large tasks by breaking them down into
manageable chunks.

★ You get more out of the meetings you choose to
attend.

★ You plan what work to do when you make a
journey.

★ You complete your activities within a given time.

4.   Ways of Saving Time

Saving time is easier than you think. It is all about getting yourself organized. There are a number of excellent, practical ways of doing this.

Making Lists

Many people think they are able to do several things at the same time. They are usually mistaken, and only end up doing things badly or not completing them at all. The secret is to do things consecutively by making lists to remind yourself what you should be doing.

Making lists is a key activity in getting organized. Your lists should reflect your priorities and contain details of what you intend to do. Writing things down is halfway to getting them done. Here are some examples of the types of lists which will help in the process of controlling time:

● Make a list of things which must be achieved today. If the list exceeds six things, you are unlikely to do them all. If an item stays on your list for more than three days, ask yourself why. The situation will either now be at crisis point, have solved itself, or was not worth doing in the first place.

- Make a list of things which you need to achieve within a limited space of time and put them into a sensible working order. That way you will feel that you are in control of events, rather than the other way round.

- When you have to leave your desk, write down what you want to do. If you get side-tracked, you can easily forget what you were going for in the first place and may return to your desk without having accomplished even one of the things you intended to do.

Many people resist the formality of writing simple things down, but memory can let you down. Research indicates that seven items (plus or minus two) are the maximum number of things that can be remembered easily.

If you are interrupted when you are carrying those items in your memory, the number of items which can be recalled becomes even less. So write down what has to be done. That way:

- You do not forget anything important.

- You do not have to make a second journey or telephone call to complete your tasks.

- You can tick off the things you have completed which will give you a real sense of achievement.

Handling Paperwork

There are several pitfalls which can prevent you from being properly organized. An untidy desk, briefcase, cupboard or car may indicate that you are unsure of how to manage yourself or your paperwork. Rather than throw anything out you keep it all. The way to deal with paperwork is to handle it once, and once only. Each time a piece of paper comes your way take action in one of the following ways:

- **File** it
- **Act** upon it
- **Pass** it on
- **Bin** it.

The last is the one that causes people the most problems because they are reluctant to take the decision to throw a piece of paper away. It is probable that the use of the bin as an organizational tool is given less importance than it should be. The squirrel instinct is endemic and not one to be encouraged if you want to manage your time more effectively. If the paper is of no use to you, be ruthless, get rid of it.

If you really cannot bring yourself to do so, then have a tray marked Fog Bound, Deep Litter, or whatever, for things which you cannot make up your mind about. After a few months, take the bottom third and, without looking at it, throw it away. If it has not become urgent by the time you do this, it cannot be all that important.

Keeping Personal Records

Knowing what has occurred on a day-to-day basis is important, especially as other people's perceptions may not be quite the same as yours. To make sure that at least you know you are right, record things as they occur by:

- **Keeping a dedicated note-book** in which you write down everything from daily reminders to the resolutions of the board meeting. Have it with you at all times.

- **Keeping paper and pens by the telephone** – it is amazing how many people do not. You find this out just as you are about to give them details of something, when they say, "Just a minute, I need to find a pen."

- **Having an index** of important names, addresses and telephone numbers readily to hand. Do not rely on the telephone's memory banks: if you are on the phone, you cannot get another number out of the system.

- **Logging important mail and telephone calls,** inwards and outwards, in your working diary, so that you know when things happened and when you responded.

Finding Things

If you have a good retrieval system, you will find things quite quickly. If your system is poor or non-existent, it is worth spending time organizing one.

Make sure you keep it simple. Few people need a complicated cross-reference system. It rarely helps you to find things any faster and requires more time to file in the first place. Sort out a system to suit your own needs and make sure you know how it works so that you can find things when you need them. Some simple filing systems are:

- Well-labelled box files for major projects.

- A tray marked 'Immediate' for each day's six tasks.

- Individual pocket folders for various topics, kept in alphabetical order.

- A concertina wallet for keeping documents in chronological order.

- A set of index cards for keeping comprehensive customer records, filed alphabetically, or by product.

- A stack of envelopes labelled by month in which you put your receipts.

- A brightly-coloured folder or box file marked 'VIP' where you put all your important bits and pieces. It needs to be brightly coloured so you never lose track of it.

Knowing exactly where you keep pieces of paper is crucial in controlling your time. But be sure that whatever is meant to go into a file is actually put there. Much of this is common sense, but it is often the small disciplines which help a great deal more with good time management than all the personal time systems and fancy wall-charts in the world.

Taking Short Cuts

Getting behind is a universal problem. Desperate measures are needed on occasions when there is simply no time to function as you usually would. For instance:

- Instead of typing a letter in response to incoming mail, write your reply on the original, make a photocopy of it and return it to the sender. (The recipient would infinitely rather get a reply, however inelegant, than one that is late, or none at all.)

- Use a compliment slip or a postcard for a quick hand-written note, instead of a typing a letter.

- Use your wastepaper basket. If something is that important and you have disposed of it in error, it will be sure to come back again.

- Time telephone calls with a 3-minute egg timer, particularly when you know the person you are calling is inclined to waffle.

Summary: Being Organized

There are many things which can get in the way of being able to manage your time efficiently. It is important to make sure that your lack of personal organization is not one of them.

Keeping tidy makes it easier to find things quickly and stops you wasting time by having to look for things in unlikely places.

Responding instantly by using emergency tactics means you will be able to make time for most things when a real log-jam has occurred.

By being personally organized, you stay in control of what you should and can control.

Questions to Ask Yourself

Think about how you organize yourself and answer the following questions:

➤ Do things stay on my 'to do' list for several days?

➤ Do I forget to do things because I did not write them down?

➤ Do I tend to temporarily lose important memos, letters and documents?

➤ Do I forget appointments or day-to-day routine activities?

➤ Do I handle paperwork several times before actioning it?

➤ Is it hard to find things when I need them in a hurry?

➤ Do I always seem to be trying to do too many things at the same time?

You Will Be Doing Better If...

★ You make lists of things you need to do.

★ You handle your paperwork only once.

★ You use the wastepaper basket with confidence.

★ You find important things in seconds rather than minutes.

★ You have a workable retrieval system that suits your needs.

★ You keep records of events.

★ You keep abreast of the deluge by taking short cuts.

★ You are considerably more confident that you have things under control.

★ You have not mislaid anything for some time.

5. Working With Others

Other people are an essential part of business, but they can be great time-wasters. Working effectively with people is part of managing your time efficiently.

When you are very busy it is tempting to say, "I'll do it myself; that way I'll make sure it gets done and I'll know it's alright."

This is fine in for a little while, when you are up against unexpectedly tight schedules. But in the long run, if you do not spend some time teaching someone else to do the task you will have burdened yourself with an unwanted extra, simply because no-one else can do it. If that task takes an hour of your time per week and if teaching someone else to do it will take a total of two to three hours, you could save yourself nearly fifty hours in the course of the year.

Delegating Work

Passing tasks on to others allows you more time for yourself. However, in the 'leaner and fitter' environment of many businesses, finding someone to pass the tasks to is often not easy.

Many people think that delegating is simply about passing work out willy-nilly and hoping that someone will do it properly. But there are some points which need to be observed if you are to ensure that tasks get done correctly and on time. You need to:

- Make sure you choose someone who is willing and able to do what needs to be done.

- Tell the person precisely what you would like done and, if necessary, how you would like the work carried out. State the time-scale for the task and indicate how often you would like a progress report.

- Assign a priority to the work being delegated so that it can be fitted in with other work which that person has to do.

- Make sure the person who is taking on the work has the authority to carry out these responsibilities. And if the work requires liaison with others, especially with senior people, make sure you 'smooth the path' for the person concerned. Above all, do not introduce anyone unprepared and unsupported into situations that may be fraught with problems such as 'company politics'.

- As well as defining the results you want, show that you care about them. If others know that you care about the task being completed successfully and on time, they will also care about achieving this.

- Regularly review progress and discuss any problems being encountered when carrying out the work – especially if you are developing a person's skills.

If you do not make it clear what is required and why, the task will be brought back to you to do all over again yourself. You may also have irretrievably upset the people you are delegating to, since they have not only failed to complete the task but they have also wasted their time.

There are two other important things to remember:

- Delegating efficiently means passing out the good things as well as the not-so-good things. It will soon be noticed if you only delegate the dreary tasks and keep all the attractive ones yourself. If this is happening, you cannot be surprised if people are reluctant to take on work from you or do not complete it on time.

- You should not delegate work which you find difficult to do yourself. If you have problems, how will other people do any better than you? This is when you should be going to someone more expert to seek assistance, not leaving someone who is not competent to struggle on, and ultimately be defeated and demoralized by the task.

Working Productively Together

Being aware of other people's time will help you to ensure that they value yours. Here are some ideas on how to maximize joint efforts:

- Make sure you pass on relevant information at the time you receive it. If others get this information too late they will have wasted their time working to the original instructions. Or they will waste your time interrupting you to ask questions.

- When you have a brilliant idea which causes you to change your mind, remember to tell others. If you do not, they will continue with previously agreed activities which may not now be relevant.

- Agree deadlines with those involved and let them know how you arrived at the timing of the deadline. Say, "We need to get this done by next Tuesday, and the reason for this is because..." You will find people more likely to get things done on time when they understand why.

- If you ask someone to work late, make sure the task is urgent and not something that could be done tomorrow. Otherwise you will have not only caused them to give up their time but they will be less willing to take on urgent work next time you ask.

Communicating Effectively

Communicating is basically about making sure other people have understood what you want them to do, and that you have understood the instructions given to you. Look at how you give instructions to others, and make sure that:

- You use clear, everyday words when giving instructions. Make sure that there is no ambiguity in what you say. This increases the chances of things being right first time. It is extraordinary how few people will take the time to do something right the first time, yet will somehow find the time to re-do it.

- On the telephone, you check that people have written down important information by asking them to repeat it back to you.

- When recording a message on your answering machine, you help people to leave a coherent message by inviting them to give not only their name and number but the time and day that they called. It is surprising how many calls are overtaken by events which, more often than not, make messages useless.

You can help others to make better use of your time by looking at how you are given instructions. For example:

- Verify that you have understood what is required and ask questions to clarify points of detail.

- Write down important information when talking on the telephone and read it back to ensure its accuracy.

- When you leave a message on an answering machine, say who you are, the day and time that you called, what your message relates to and a current contact telephone number.

The disciplines involved in effective communication are worth the time spent on them. They prevent the time-wasting aggravation of having to unravel misunderstandings. Communicating properly contributes considerably to making the best possible use of your time.

Having Work Delegated to You

Working with others involves managing their time as well as your own. If other people are disorganized, they can waste your time. So you have to help them to make better use of your time and theirs by discussing with them:

- Why the work has to be done.

- What is wanted – precisely.

- When the work is required.

- What form the work should take.

Knowing why the work is needed can give valuable clues as to what has to be done. If the work is for internal use, a rough draft may be enough. Being able to focus on the end-receiver helps prevent time being wasted in providing the wrong sort of information. Knowing in what form it is required is even better. Producing a 5-page report when a verbal briefing would have done is clearly a waste of time.

Work out if what you have been asked to do fits in with your priorities. This way, you can make a sensible assessment as to whether what is requested can be fitted in without detracting from your own activities. If you do not find out, you can be laden with work not of your own making, and may be unable to complete any of it satisfactorily. You may be seen as a busy person, but also as one who is unable to get anything done on time.

Summary: Sharing Time

Helping others to help you make better use of your time is an essential part of managing your time well.

Delegating work can save you time if you make sure people know what they are doing, but you need to communicate properly and spend a little time ensuring that they are quite clear about what is required of them.

Equally, when you take on work you need to clarify exactly what it is that you are expected to do. More often than not others neglect to inform you sufficiently about what is required and you could waste valuable time doing what you think is needed rather than what actually is.

It is alarming how much time is wasted repeating tasks unnecessarily. So it is never a waste of time to check that you have fully understood what is needed. Making certain of the facts means that everyone makes better use of their time.

Questions to Ask Yourself

Assess how well you are making the best use of your time and other people's by answering the following questions:

➤ Do I delegate enough?

➤ Do I follow the 'rules' when passing out work?

➤ Do I always indicate that I care about the results of the tasks I delegate?

➤ Do I make sure that if I require urgent work from someone, it does have to be done immediately and not tomorrow?

➤ Do I give clear instructions about what has to be done and why?

➤ Do I always make sure that I have fully understood what is required of me?

➤ Have I taken the time to check anything that is not clear so that the task does not have to be done all over again?

You Will Be Doing Better If...

★ You delegate certain tasks instead of doing them all yourself.

★ You follow the guidelines when delegating.

★ You pass out interesting tasks and routine tasks in equal proportions.

★ You prevent someone else from wasting your time and theirs.

★ You communicate clearly and you check that you are properly understood.

★ You verify what is required of you before you go ahead and do it.

★ You cannot think of anything you have done recently which has wasted other people's time.

6. Making Time for Yourself

Getting your work done and accommodating others takes up most of your time, so it is easy to find yourself last in the line for attention. By examining the ways you use time in your personal life, you may see how you could put yourself at the head of the queue.

Revising Your Personal Habits

Think of everything you do from the time you wake up in the morning. Work out how your personal routine may be losing you time and think what you have to do to change your behaviour. For example:

- If you hang your clothes on the floor, you will have to spend a lot more time getting those garments ready to wear another day.

- If you are still using the same route you took to work on your first day, you will not have explored other options. There are probably several other ways which may be quicker or better on certain days. You won't know until you try.

- If you are having to go some distance for certain services, you could find a company that collects and delivers.

Taking Leisure Time

Make sure you schedule your leisure time otherwise you will never get any. This is particularly critical if you work for yourself. It may seem a bit extreme to schedule time off, but if work expands to fill the time, it is easy to see how you can miss out.

You may already be caught in a well-known trap – on the one hand feeling that you should be working whenever you take a little time off; on the other hand working long hours with no let-up and feeling slightly resentful that while others lead full social lives, you never seem to be able to.

The way out of the conundrum is simple. Give yourself permission to take time off.

There are a number of excellent ways to do this:

- Block out your holiday period in advance, so that you cannot be coerced into working instead.

- Make a contract with yourself to take off specific periods of time. For instance, Saturday is your day off, but Sunday afternoon is for catching up.

- Make time in each day to do something that is a complete contrast from work.

Making time for leisure is just as important to your efficiency as work is. It allows you to refresh your mental faculties and your physical performance.

It also means that your family and friends see you from time to time. Support from them enables you to keep things in perspective. Similarly they need support from you, and if you never make time for them, a time may come when they may not be there for you.

It is vital to your well-being, and therefore to your working ability, to make time for pleasure and personal relationships. It makes sense to remind yourself that there is not much point in allowing work to take up all your time if you have no opportunity to enjoy the rewards which come from it.

Summary: The Knock-on Effect

Your private life is not so separate from your working life as you may think. If you can take time to revise some of your personal habits, it could help you to find the time to do more.

It is vital you build time into your busy schedule to re-energize and to enjoy the benefits that your efforts in managing time better will undoubtedly bring.

Questions to Ask Yourself

Think about how you can make more time. Answer the following questions:

➤ Are there any personal habits I can change to make more use of my time?

➤ Are there any things I do simply because I always have?

➤ Do I spend time on myself?

➤ Do I have specific time set aside for activities that have nothing whatsoever to do with work?

➤ Am I taking time to enjoy the fruits of my labours?

You Will Be Doing Better If...

★ You revise some of your personal habits to prevent yourself from wasting time.

★ You manage your time, rather than letting time managing you.

★ You do not let work take you over, but actively schedule time off from work for your own pursuits.

★ You are no longer feeling guilty that you should be working when you are not.

★ You are able to place yourself if not actually at the head of the queue, very near it.

Check List for Making Time

If you find that making better use of your time is proving to be harder than you thought, check how you are tackling these key areas:

Use of Time

If you are constantly running out of time, it could be that you have not fully analysed the use you make of your time. Knowing how you use your time provides an important baseline against which to measure the improvements you have made.

Priorities

If you are not absolutely sure of your priorities, you may find you have been doing time-consuming things which have not contributed very much to your effectiveness. Make sure you know where your priorities lie and stick to them.

Personal Organization

If you cannot find things and are personally disorganized, it may be that you need to change your habits. Changing a routine is not easy, but if you take time to examine your work and home life, you will inevitably find a number of ways you can save time.

Planning Time

If you have not developed strategies for using the time you have available to your advantage, you could be finding that you are overwhelmed by events or are wasting time because, say, you did not bring appropriate documents with you on your train journey. It is vital to plan what you want to achieve in any given situation, or you will find that you are constantly wasting precious time.

Delegating

If you are still doing everything yourself, perhaps you are not using other people's talents to best effect. Others can be of considerable help in allowing you to use your time better. If you take a little time to delegate to them properly, you can also help them to develop their own skills and thus save you time in the future.

Taking Time for Yourself

If you find that work keeps getting on top of you, and you lack energy to cope, you need to consider whether you are taking enough time to unwind from work. Scheduling leisure time for yourself to regain energy allows you to work hard and play hard.

The Benefits of Making Time

You have to want to make better use of your time. If you take managing time seriously and try to put into practice some of the ideas that have been suggested, you should find yourself less hard-pressed and with more time at your disposal.

When this happens, you will be able to put the time gained to good use in various ways by:

- Planning more thoroughly.

- Creating new ideas or starting new projects.

- Developing your skills.

- Taking care of yourself.

- Fostering personal interests.

Managing your time better can usually be achieved by thinking about the possible courses of action open to you rather than rushing directly into action.

Planning and thinking are activities which people do not always see as being 'real' work. You must learn to label it as real work, and even periodically let others know that you think it important to spend time in this way. If they see how much value you place on your time, they might even be inspired to manage their own time better.

If you are saying to yourself, "This is all very well, but it cannot be as easy as that", nobody says that trying to manage your time is easy. Some days things will go well for you and you will feel you have achieved a great deal. On other days, events will overcome you and all your best-laid plans will fall apart. You must not give up, saying that it is all too difficult, but determine to try again the next day.

Remember the Chinese Emperor's cedars and start right now.

Glossary

Here are some definitions in relation to Making Time.

Attitude – Entrenched view that can influence the way you get things done.

Being effective – Ensuring that the right things get done.

Being efficient – Ensuring that things get done in the right way. The classic way to waste time is to be very efficient but also totally ineffective.

Competence – Ability to do something efficiently and effectively and thus save time.

Crises – Time-wasting happenings which could have been prevented, but which have now reached panic proportions.

Deadlines – Fixed points that limit the amount of time available to waste.

Delegating – Passing on the right things to the right people.

Diary – The simplest tool ever devised for personal organization.

Excuses – Very poor reasons for not doing something.

Important – Something that matters; not the same thing as 'Urgent'.

Organizing – Ensuring that you make maximum use of resources when time is at a premium.

Priorities – What you must do, rather than what you would like to do.

Responsibilities – Issues for which you are entirely accountable, usually too many.

Retrieval system – Cunning method of making sure you find something quickly the next time you need it.

Squirrel instinct – Hiding your nuts so well that you can't find them again.

Urgent – That which needs doing within a tight time-frame, not necessarily important.

Wasted time – Opportunities which will never recur.

The Author

Kate Keenan is a Chartered Occupational Psychologist with degrees in affiliated subjects (B.Sc., M.Phil.) and a number of qualifications in others.

She founded Keenan Research, an industrial psychology consultancy, in 1978. The work of the consultancy is fundamentally concerned with helping people to achieve their potential and make a better job of their management.

By devising work programmes for companies she enables them to target and remedy their managerial problems – from personnel selection and individual assessment to team building and attitude surveys. She believes in giving priority to training the managers to institute their own programmes, so that their company resources are developed and expanded.

Having learned the hard way that it is always later than one thinks, she now enjoys helping others to manage their time sooner than she did.

THE MANAGEMENT GUIDES

Available now at £2.99 each:

Making Time ☐

Managing ☐

Managing Yourself ☐

Planning ☐

Selecting People ☐

Solving Problems ☐

To be published in July 1995:

Communicating ☐

Delegating ☐

Meetings ☐

Motivating ☐

Negotiating ☐

Understanding Behaviour ☐

These books are available at your local bookshop or newsagent, or can be ordered direct. Prices and availability are subject to change without notice. Just tick the titles you require and send a cheque or postal order for the value of the book to:

B.B.C.S., P.O. Box 941, HULL HU1 3VQ (24 hour Telephone Credit Card Line: 01482 224626), and add for postage & packing:

UK (& BFPO) Orders: £1.00 for the first book & 50p for each additional book up to a maximum of £2.50.
Overseas (& Eire) Orders: £2.00 for the first book, £1.00 for the second & 50p for each additional book.